THE NOVELLO
BARBERSHOP
SONGBOOK

Arranged by
Nicholas Hare

This book © Novello Publishing Limited
14-15 Berners Street, London W1T 3LJ
Order No. NOV 072457
ISBN 0-7119-3013-9

Music processed by New Notations

Preface

The Novello Barbershop Songbook,
offers unaccompanied arrangements of a variety of
well-loved songs, from the 40s to the 70s.

The arranger has endeavoured to share the interest
amongst all the voice parts, but each singer should be aware at
all times of who has the melody, so that it is allowed to stand out.
A discreet use of soloists is often appropriate:
some suggestions are given.

Blend and balance of the harmony is another vital element
in successful performance of this music, and vibrato should
be kept in check, so that the chords are clean and perfectly in tune.
The various 'vocalisations' (ah, ooh, mm, etc.) may be
considered as suggestions only and varied according
to the performance conditions.

Also new from Novello:

Novello Voices
Three new series of great songs, superbly arranged
for choirs and close-harmony groups:
Choral Suites – Concert suites from hit musicals
Show Singles – West End and Broadway show-stoppers
Choral Pops – Classic chart hits

Novello Publishing Limited

Performance Notes

Angel Eyes
PAGE 4

This beautiful bluesy number needs careful handling. At this slow tempo it is very important to keep a steady beat to provide a structure against which the individual voices can interpret their swung rhythms with a certain freedom. The accompanying singers should sustain their lines with quiet intensity.

Eleanor Rigby
PAGE 8

The accompanying parts should be neat and tidy, with no let-up in the rhythm until the final bar. It is particularly important that the lyrics should be clearly projected.

The Girl From Ipanema
PAGE 11

Sing this Latin-American number with a strong sense of rhythm, even in the smoother sections.

Maria
PAGE 14

Take care over the tuning, particularly at the change of key at Bar 9, where the pervasive tritone D-G# is prominent, and in the final section.
The last 'Maria', which needs great control, could be given to a soloist.

Satin Doll
PAGE 17

The close harmony in this song needs a smooth balance between the parts. If you have enough voices, try the rich chords in the alternative final bar. The rhythms should be gently swung.

Swing Low, Sweet Chariot
PAGE 20

In this arrangement, the melody migrates from voice to voice: make the joins smooth, without too many differences in tone.

Uptown Girl
PAGE 23

Sing Billy Joel's confident number with gusto. The second bass part frequently provides an important rhythmic backing.

Wake Up, Little Susie
PAGE 28

This song is from the same year as 'Uptown Girl' and requires the same bright approach. The opening should simulate strumming guitars. Keep a strict beat from beginning to end.

What I Did For Love
PAGE 33

The expressive melody in the first bass may be treated with some freedom against the steady, accurate beat of the backing provided by other voices.

When I'm Sixty Four
PAGE 37

Make sure that these delightful words are heard clearly and not obscured by accompaniment, which once again should be very rhythmic.

Whispering Grass
PAGE 42

There are some touches of close harmony in this Fisher classic. Work for a smooth, balanced blend.

Yesterday
PAGE 46

This is another case where the melody may be treated quite freely, provided that the accompanying parts provide a clear beat.

ANGEL EYES

Words by Earl Brent
Music by Matt Dennis
arr. Nicholas Hare

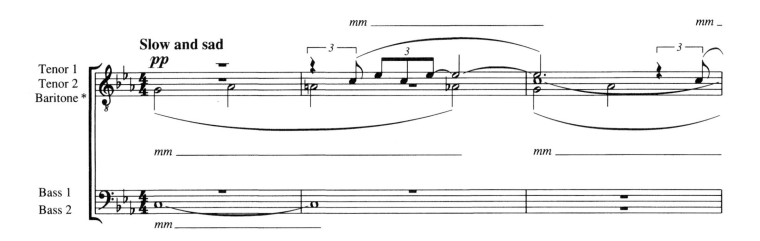

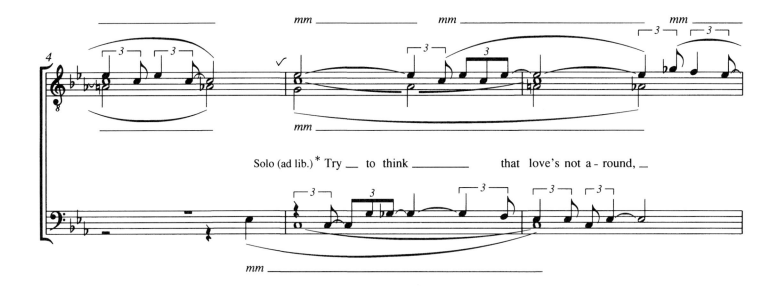

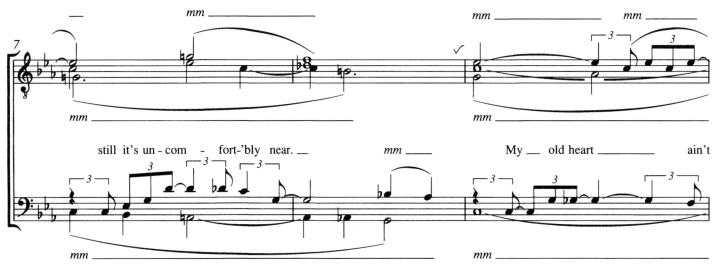

* If the melody is sung by a soloist, the rest of the first basses may sing the baritone part.

ELEANOR RIGBY

Words and Music by
John Lennon and Paul McCartney
arr Nicholas Hare

Moderately, with a steady beat

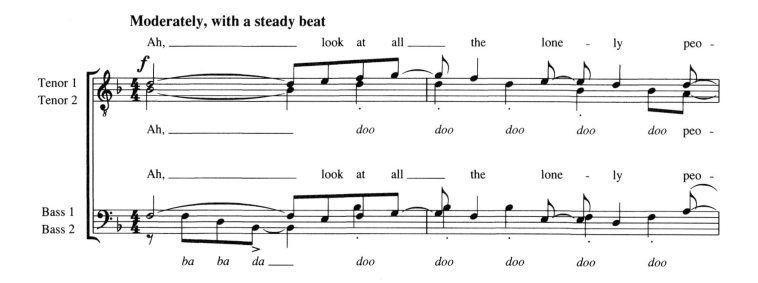

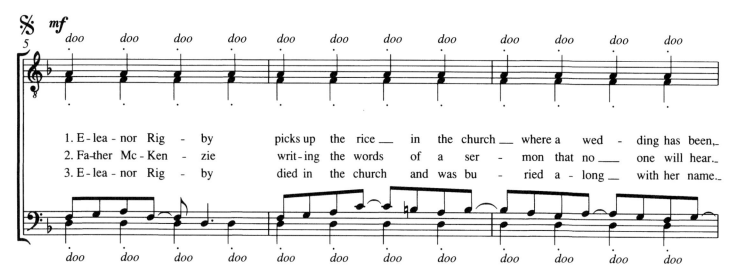

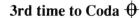

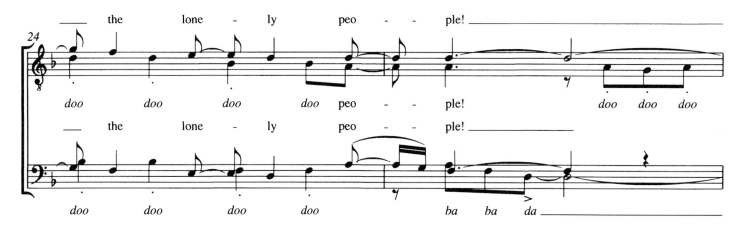

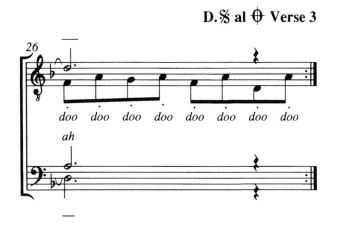

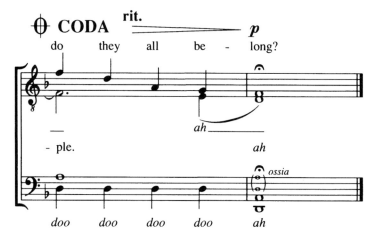

THE GIRL FROM IPANEMA
(Garota De Ipanema)

Music by Antonio Carlos Jobim
English words by Norman Gimbel
Original words by Vinicius de Moraes
arr. Nicholas Hare

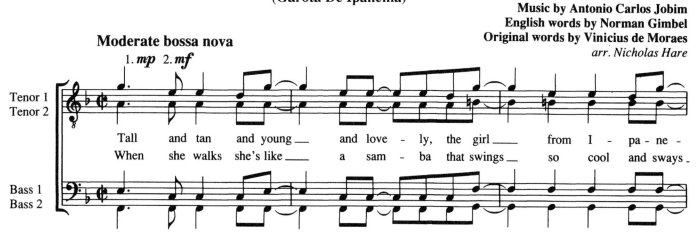

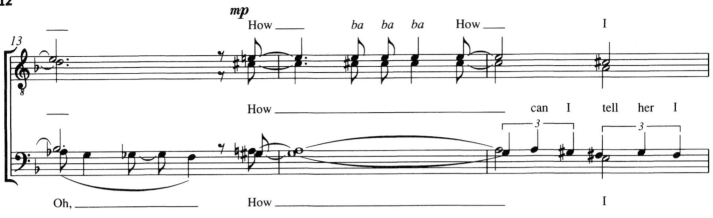

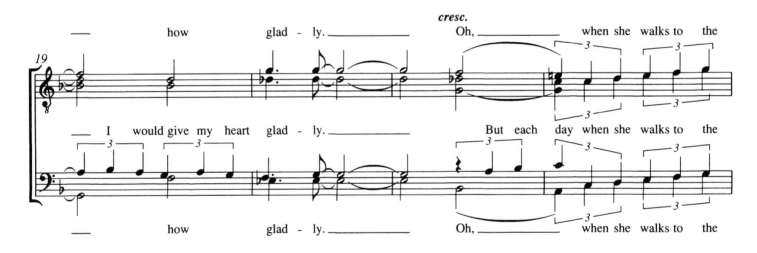

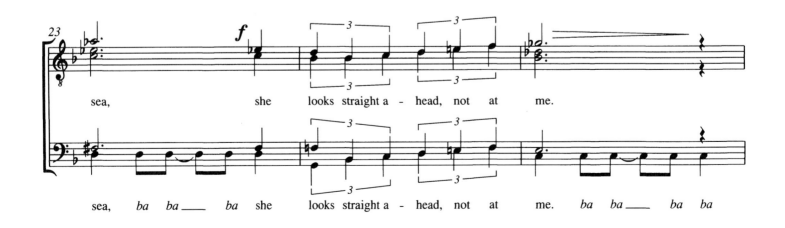

* optional additional notes printed small.

MARIA

from *West Side Story*

Words by Stephen Sondheim
Music by Leonard Bernstein
arr. Nicholas Hare

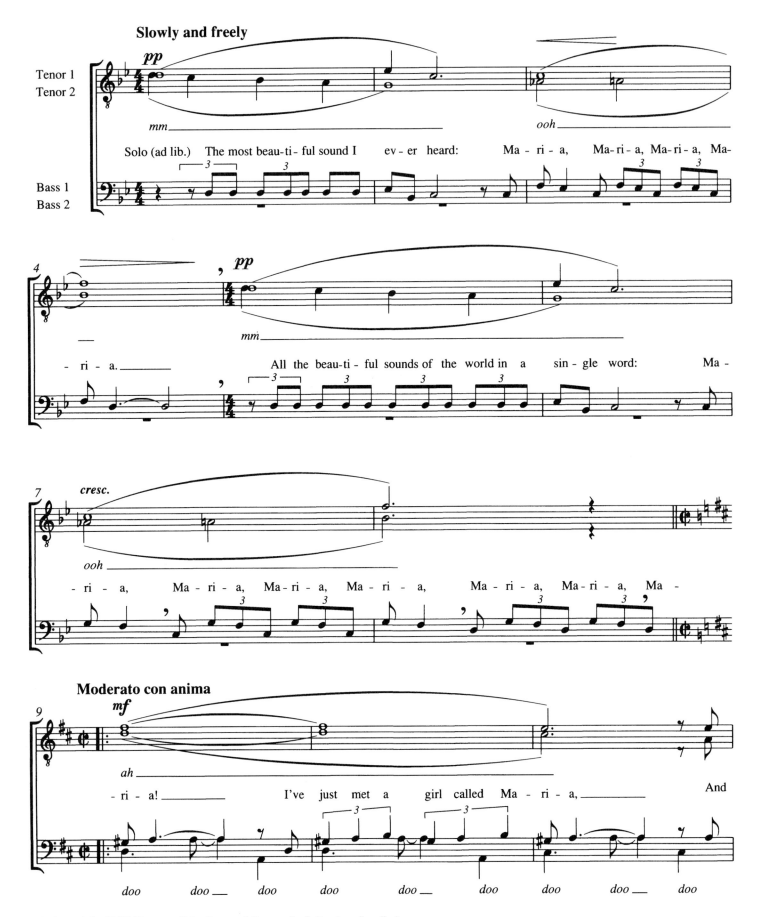

sud - den - ly that name, Will ne - ver be the same to me.

Ma -

doo *doo* *doo* *doo* *doo* *doo* *doo* *doo* *doo*

cresc.

ah

- ri - a! I've just kissed a girl named Ma - ri - a, And

doo *doo* *doo* *doo* *doo* *doo* *doo* *doo* *doo*

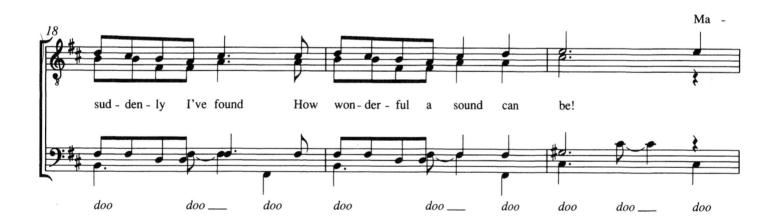

Ma -

sud - den - ly I've found How won - der - ful a sound can be!

doo *doo* *doo* *doo* *doo* *doo* *doo* *doo* *doo*

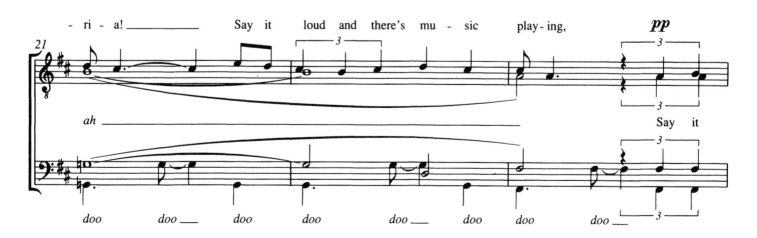

- ri - a! Say it loud and there's mu - sic play - ing,

pp

ah

Say it

doo *doo* *doo* *doo* *doo* *doo* *doo* *doo*

SATIN DOLL

Words by Johnny Mercer
Music by Duke Ellington & Billy Strayhorn
arr. Nicholas Hare

Moderately, with a beat

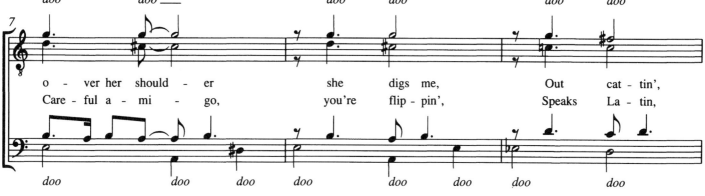

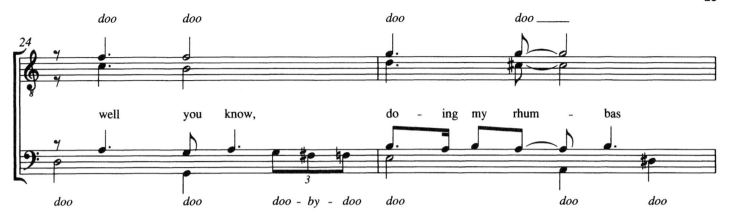

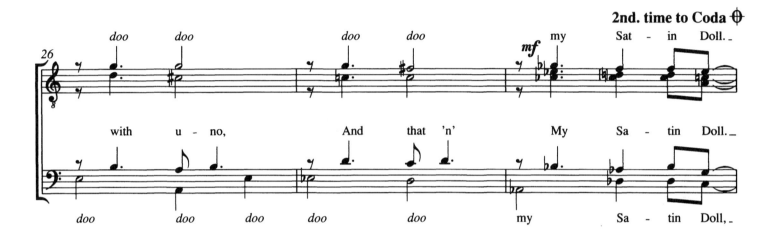

2nd. time to Coda ⊕

D.%. al Coda

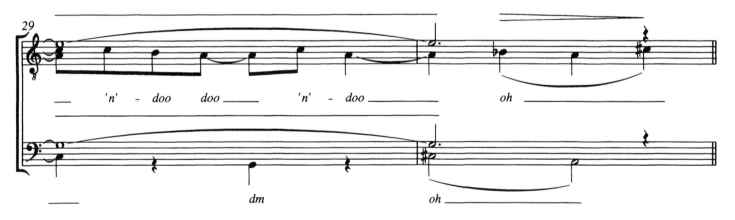

⊕ **CODA**

Alternative final bar

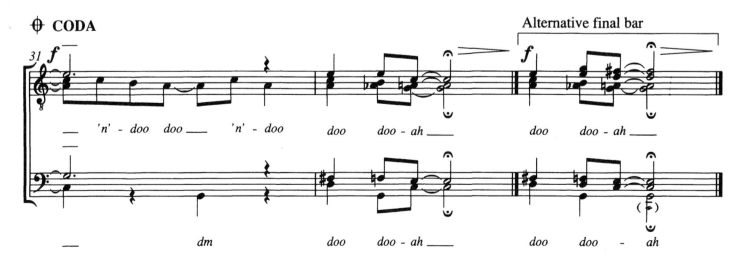

SWING LOW, SWEET CHARIOT

American Spiritual
arr. Nicholas Hare

UPTOWN GIRL

Words and Music by Billy Joel
arr. Nicholas Hare

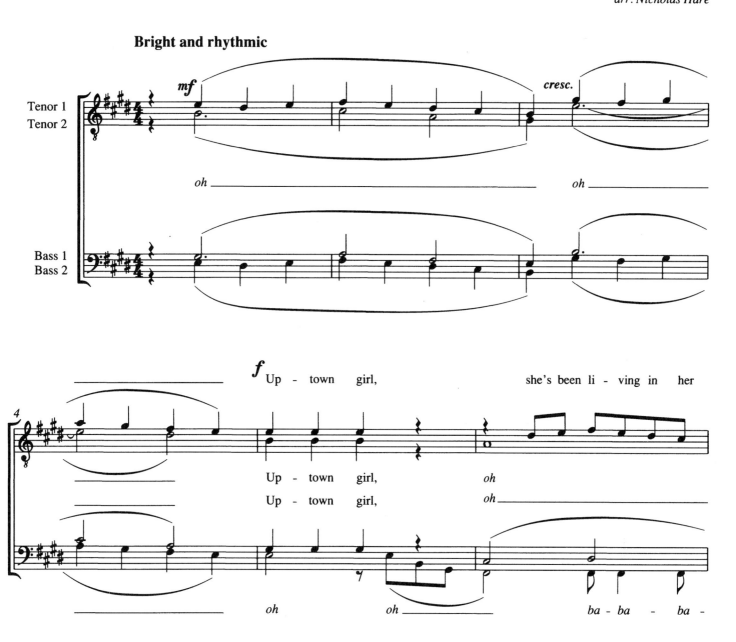

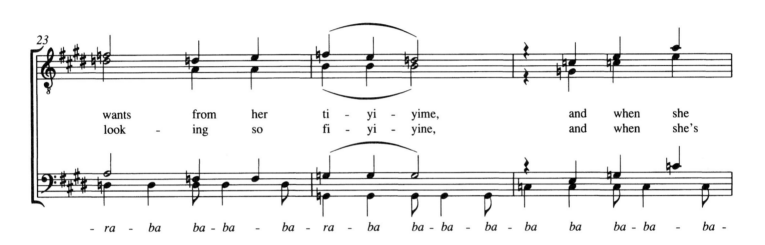

- ra - ba ba - ba - ba - ra - ba ba - ba - ba - ra - ba ba ba

oh
oh
ba ba ba - ba - ba - ra - ba ba - ba - ba - ra - ba ba - ba - ba -

up - town girl, _____ She's my up - town

up - town girl,
up - town girl,
oh _____
- ra - ba ba - ba - ba oh oh _____ ba - ba - ba -

girl, _____ oh _____ (Original repeats to fade) Optional ending after repeat (remaining *f*)

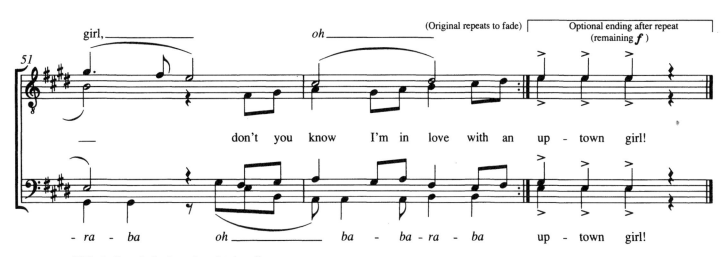

don't you know I'm in love with an up - town girl!
- ra - ba oh _____ ba - ba - ra - ba up - town girl!

* Falsetto if required - alternative printed small

WAKE UP LITTLE SUSIE

Words and Music by
Felice and Boudleaux Bryant
arr. Nicholas Hare

Bright rock tempo

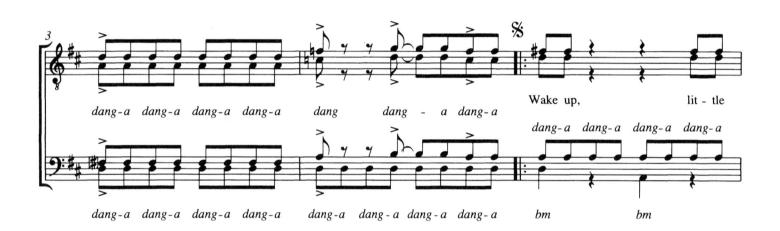

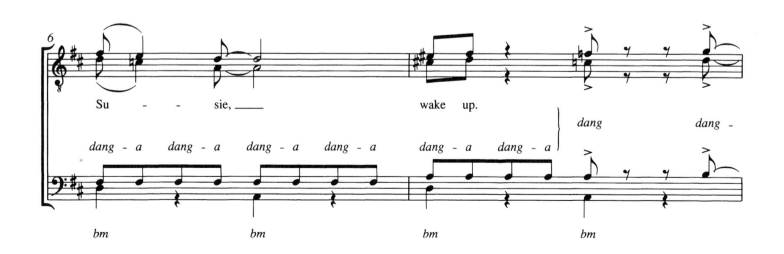

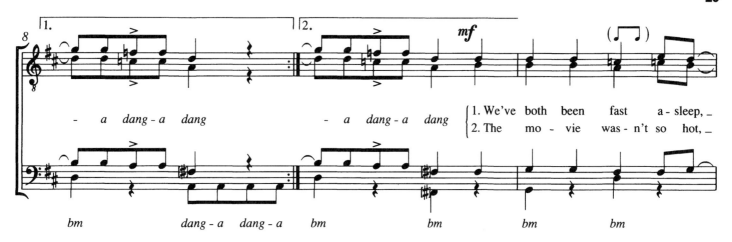

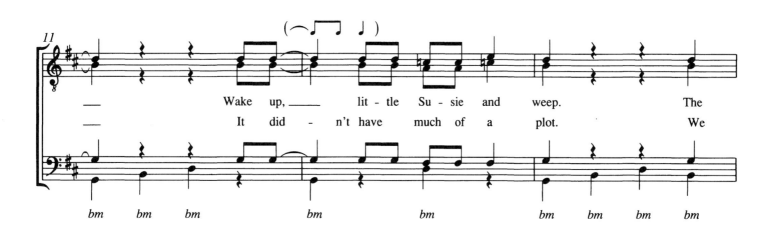

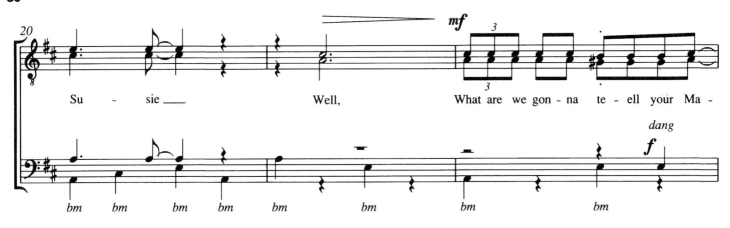

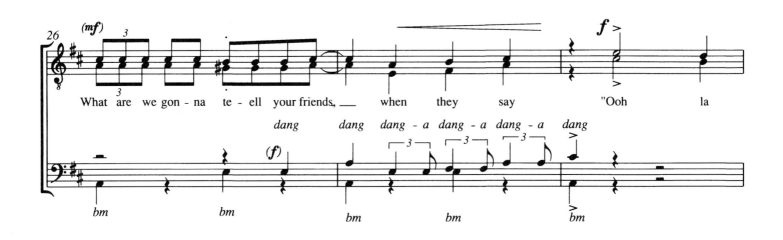

2nd time to CODA ⊕

mf

Su - - sie. _____ ooh _____

ba ba ba ba ba ba ba Well, we told your Ma - ma that

ba ba ba ba bm bm

we'd be in by ten. Well,

bm bm bm ba - da _____ ba - da da bm bm bm

ooh _____

Su - sie, ba - by, looks like we goofed a - gain _____

bm bm bm bm bm bm bm

f

Wake up, _____ lit - tle Su - sie, _____ Wake up _____ lit - tle

bm bm bm bm bm bm bm bm bm bm bm bm

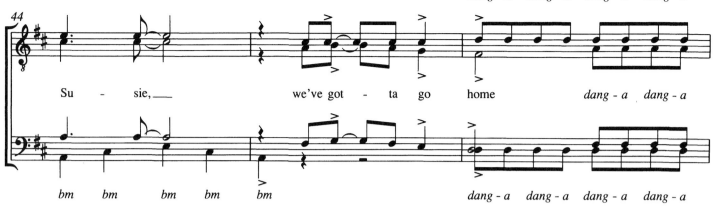

WHAT I DID FOR LOVE

from *A Chorus Line*

Words by Edward Kleban
Music by Marvin Hamlisch
arr. Nicholas Hare

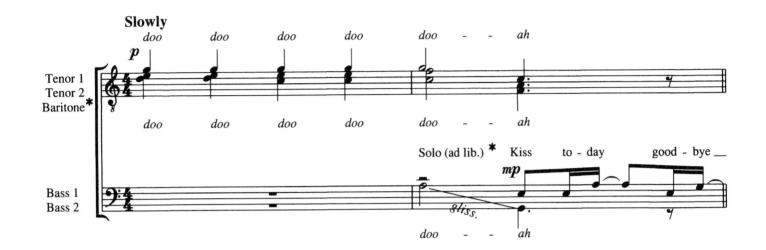

* If the melody is sung by a soloist, the rest of the first basses may sing the baritone part.

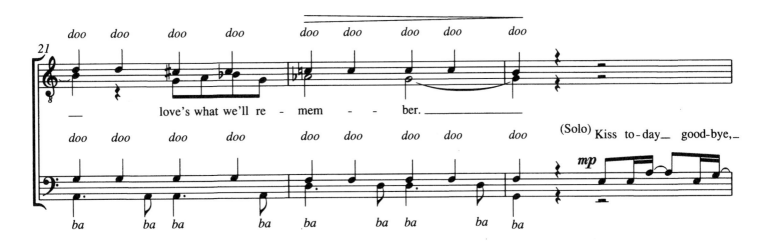

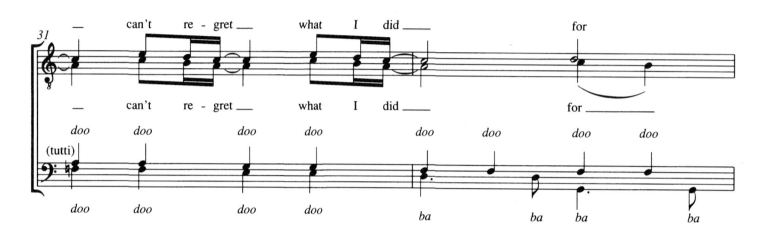

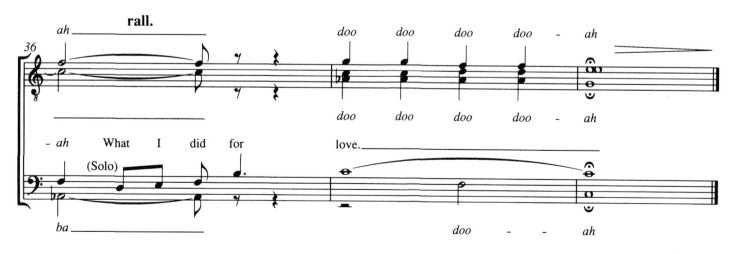

WHEN I'M SIXTY FOUR

Words and Music by
John Lennon and Paul McCartney
arr. Nicholas Hare

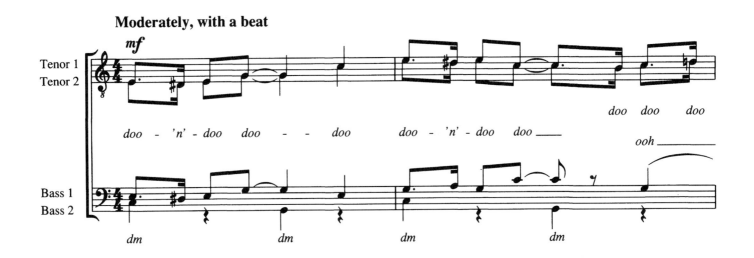

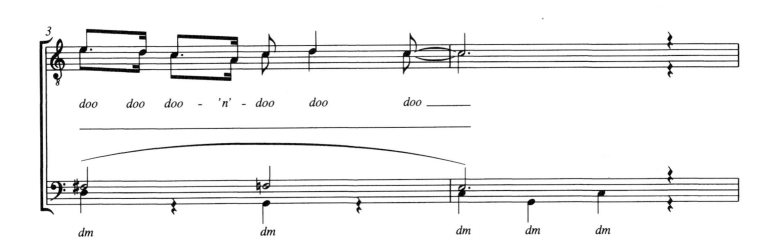

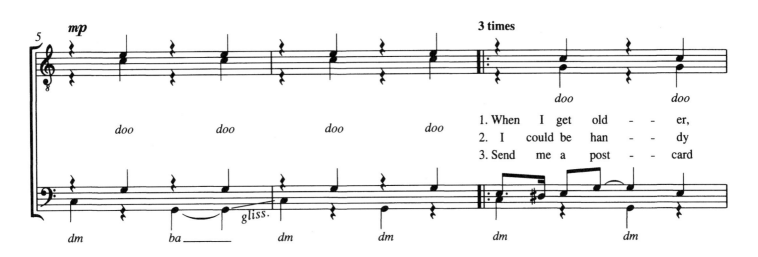

CODA
cresc.

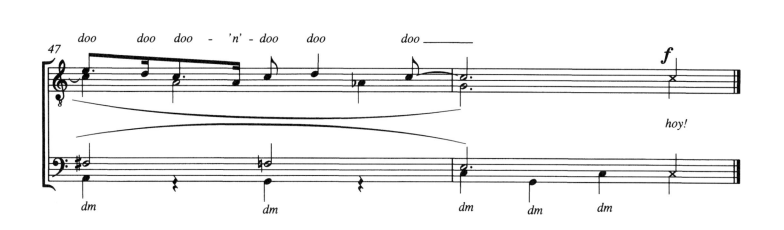

WHISPERING GRASS
(Don't Tell The Trees)

Words by Fred Fisher
Music by Doris Fisher
arr. Nicholas Hare

44

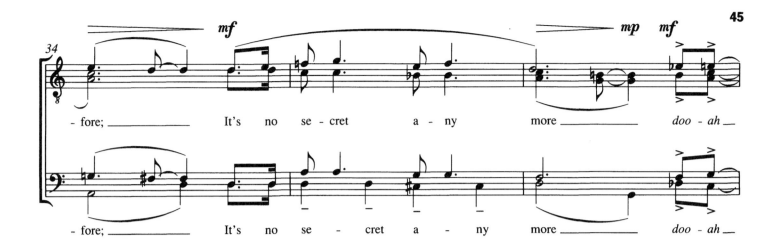

-fore; _____ It's no se-cret a-ny more _____ *doo - ah* __

-fore; _____ It's no se-cret a-ny more _____ *doo - ah* __

_ Why tell them all the old things? They're bu-ried un-der the

_ *bom bom bom bom bom bom bom*

snow. Whis-per-ing grass, __ don't tell the trees 'cause the

snow. *ah* _____ 'cause the

trees don't need to know __ No, no! __ *doo - ah* __ No, no! __

trees don't need to know __ No, no! __ *doo - ah* __ No, no! __

YESTERDAY

**Words and Music by
John Lennon and Paul McCartney**

arr. Nicholas Hare

After verse 4 to Coda

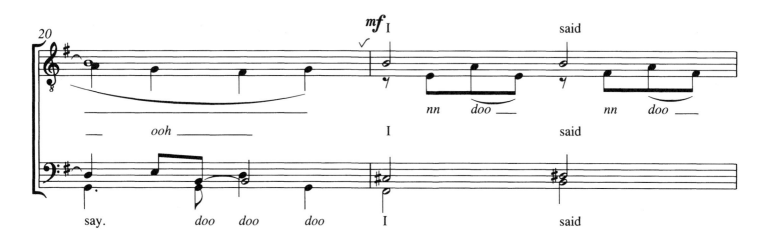

2nd time D.𝄋 al Coda

⊕ CODA

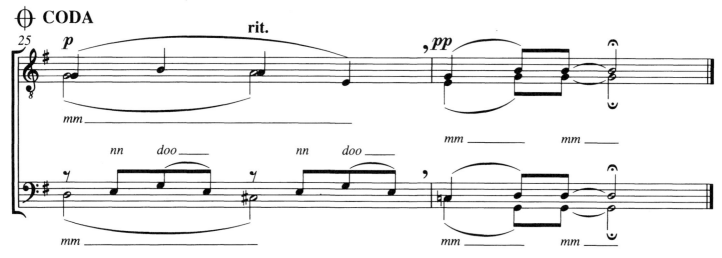